be a winner in
ICE HOCKEY

By the Same Author

Aerospace Pilot
Aerospace Power, *a Pictorial Guide*
Auto Racing
Be a Winner in Baseball
Bicycling
Bush Flying in Alaska
Cleared for Takeoff, *Behind the Scenes at an Airport*
Deep-Sea World, *the Story of Oceanography*
Drag Racing
Gateway to Space
Motorcycling
Project Apollo, *Mission to the Moon*
Project Mercury
Rockets, Missiles, and Moons
Skyhooks, *the Story of Helicopters*
Skylab
Skyrocketing Into the Unknown
Spacetrack, *Watchdog of the Skies*

be a winner in
ICE HOCKEY

BY CHARLES COOMBS

illustrated with 57 photographs and diagrams
William Morrow and Company
New York 1974

Library of Congress Cataloging in Publication Data
Coombs, Charles Ira (date)
  Be a winner in ice hockey.

  1. Hockey—Juvenile literature. I. Title.
GV847.25.C66 1974   796.9′62   73-10769
ISBN 0-688-20099-0
ISBN 0-688-30099-5 (lib. bdg.)

Printed in the United States of America.
1   2   3   4   5   78   77   76   75   74

Acknowledgments for Photographs
Paul Bereswill, New York Islanders, page 51; Cooper International, Inc., pages 12, 21, 110; Sam Kushner/Philadelphia Flyers, pages 10, 79, 112, 117; Minnesota North Stars, pages 67, 115; Ron Moscati/Buffalo Sabres, pages 42, 63, 65; Manny Rubio/Atlanta Flames, pages 25, 27; Al Ruelle/Boston Bruins, pages 28, 29, 53, 64, 88, 89, 103, 107, 108, 113; David Schofield/Buffalo Sabres, pages 105, 122; Elwood Smith/Philadelphia Flyers, pages 75, 77, 83; Richard Titley/Philadelphia Flyers, page 116; Toronto Maple Leafs, page 41; U.S. Air Force Academy, pages 16, 44; Vancouver Canucks, page 85.
  All other photographs were taken by the author.

contents

1. The Game 9

2. Skating 24

3. Quick with the Stick 34

4. Passing 46

5. Shot on Goal 60

6. On Offense 72

7. On Defense 87

8. The Man in the Mask 106

9. The Hat Trick 119

Glossary 123

Index 126

*To Frank Bonham,
in remembrance of the many times,
hidden away in a high mountain cabin,
that we have laughed and agonized
while working on our separate books.*

chapter one
THE GAME

Ice hockey is the fastest team sport in the world. It is an exciting, demanding, and rugged game. In order to play it, you need a variety of skills all of which can be gained through hard effort and steady practice.

You must, of course, first of all be a good ice skater. But there is a lot more to playing ice hockey than just being able to stay upright on skates. Even as you race down the ice, you must stop and start, weave and dodge, circle and pivot to avoid the fierce body checks of opposing players bent upon knocking you loose from your skates. You must duck under and jump over swinging sticks that flash like sabers around you.

While doing all of this, you must also keep control of a skittish little disc that skids, bounces, and rolls at the end of your stick. If you don't have the puck, you must stay alert for a pass from a teammate or attempt to steal the puck from an opponent.

There is more to ice hockey than merely skating.

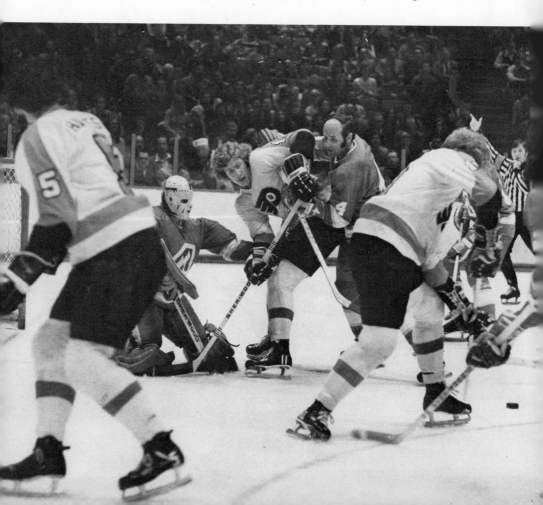

The game of ice hockey may sound like the "Charge of the Light Brigade" or a destruction derby, but hockey is no rougher than football, soccer, or water polo, if it is played right. Its speed, slippery footing, banging bodies, and swinging sticks just make it seem so.

Where did this breathless, colorful game begin? No one is sure. Thousands of years ago the Persians played something like it. And a game called "bandy," resembling hockey, was played in England in the early 1500's. At about the same time, the Irish developed a similar game in which a heavy brass ball and skull-cracking clubs were used. Farther north, the Scots played a bruising stick-and-ball game that they called, and still call, "shinny."

In the mid-1700's, explorers along the Saint Lawrence River came upon bands of young Iroquois Indians playing a game not unlike field hockey, but playing it on ice. The explorers noted that every time a young brave got walloped with a stick he yelped "ho-gee," his native version of "ouch." Some sports historians believe that "hogee" eventually became our word "hockey."

In any case, the modern game of ice hockey developed on the frozen rivers, lakes, and ponds of Canada. Today Canada remains the source of many of the world's finest hockey men, although the United States and other countries of the world produce a steadily increasing number of highly skilled players.

One day in 1875 in Montreal, Canada, two teams of nine men each tangled ferociously in the world's

Children start playing street hockey early, or joining local youth league teams.

first organized game of ice hockey. Interest in the game grew. But the eighteen players proved to be too many, so the number was cut to seven per team, and finally to the present six: a center and two wingmen (forwards), two defensemen, and a goalkeeper (goalie, goaltender, netminder).

For a long time ice hockey was played only in the northlands where ice was plentiful during much of the year. But as rinks of artificial ice surface were built, the popularity of the game spread.

Finally, in 1917, ice hockey went professional with the formation of the National Hockey League. From the original four teams, all Canadian, the NHL has continued to expand. Much later the World Hockey Association added many teams. Today there are more than two dozen first-rank professional hockey teams playing throughout Canada and the United States, with most clubs located in the States.

In addition, players are tangling on thousands of other teams: in the lesser pro circuits, in semipro, college, and junior leagues, and right on down to the growing hordes of minor leaguers, starting with five- to eight-year-old Mighty Mites and even less experienced Pollywogs. Hockey leagues now reach from the frigid regions of Canada to the tropic climes of southern United States.

Ice hockey is such a fast game and the action seems so confused that many people feel it is difficult to understand. However, ice hockey is basically like any other stick-and-ball type of game. The object is simply to advance a hard rubber disc (instead of a ball) down the ice and shoot it into the opponent's goal for a score. The team that scores most often in an hour wins.

Of course, rules govern just how the puck may or may not be advanced, varying somewhat with the ages of the players and the types of teams playing. But the basic rules and regulations are standard everywhere. Since professional hockey rules are the most basic of all, this book will deal with that level of play.

The official hockey rink is 200 feet long by 85 feet wide, although dimensions may vary where such ice space is not available. The rink is enclosed by a four-foot-high wooden fence or wall, called the "boards." The corners of the rink are rounded to enable players to carom, or bank, the puck around the end of the playing surface. At better rinks the boards are topped by shatterproof glass barriers to protect the fans from

14   *Opposite:* The official hockey rink

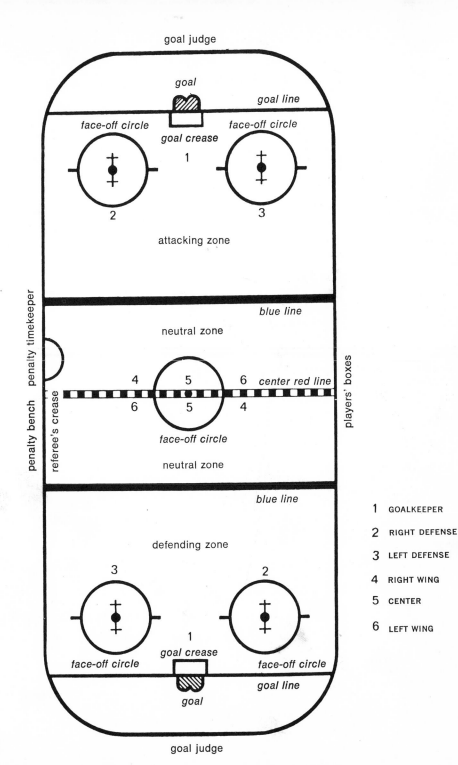

flying pucks that sometimes travel at speeds in excess of 100 miles per hour!

The ice surface is divided into three major zones. The two end zones should be sixty feet long. The center, or neutral, zone may also be sixty feet long, or it may be somewhat shorter.

In one end zone is located the goal that your team must protect—your defending zone. Your opponent's goal is at the opposite end of the rink—your attacking zone.

These two end zones are separated from the central zone by broad blue lines across the ice. Through the

An official goal—in use

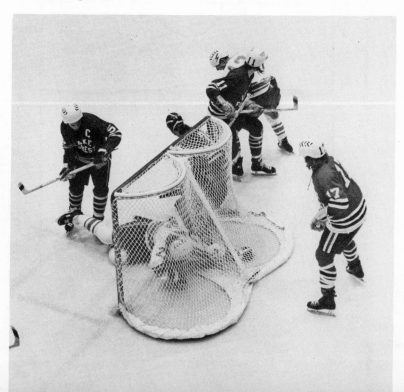

middle of the central zone runs a red line, usually dotted or broken, that divides the rink in half.

Other narrower red lines located approximately ten feet in from the end boards mark the goal lines. At the center of each goal line is the goal itself: a cage with a rectangular mouth four feet high and six feet wide. Behind the goal mouth is a net to catch the puck when a goal is scored.

In front of the goal is a four-by-eight-foot area called the "crease," which extends four feet out from the goal line and reaches a foot beyond each goalpost. *The goalie is the only person on the ice allowed to occupy the crease.*

In the center of the rink and in both end zones are face-off circles. Face-offs, or draws, are similar to the jump in basketball and are used to begin each period or after play has been whistled dead. In a face-off two opposing players square off and grapple with their sticks for possession of the puck. Most often, face-offs come as a result of zone infractions. Such infractions are probably the aspect of the game most confusing to the beginner. The whistle blows: someone has broken a rule. What rule? He only passed the puck the length of the rink, didn't he?

Exactly! And you can't do that. Otherwise, ice hockey would be the kind of wild and unmanageable melee that had the Indians yelling "ho-gee!" So, to prevent injury and chaos, the puck must be moved down the ice in controlled stages—one zone at a time.

This means you may not race down the rink to take a rink-long pass from a teammate and dash for the goal. Instead, you may rag, or stickhandle, the puck down the ice, *keeping control of it as you cross the various lines.* Or you may take a pass from a teammate *before* crossing into the attacking zone.

But the puck must go first! *It must always cross the opposing team's blue line ahead of every member of the attacking team.*

The stick handler himself will be off side if he gets too far ahead of the puck—if *both* skates are over the blue line before the puck has crossed it. When this occurs, play is stopped and the puck is faced off. (It doesn't matter where your body or stick is—your skates determine whether or not you are off side.)

Basically, then, you stay behind the puck, working it zone by zone up the ice. There is an exception, however, for the defending team. While in his own defending zone, a player may pass to a teammate all the way out to the center line without incurring an off-side penalty. But the pass must be completed before the puck reaches the center line, or an offside is called, which means another face-off and the risk of losing possession of the puck.

Another tactic that may incur a penalty is the one known as "icing." This means trying to fire it out of danger all the way down the rink and across the opponent's goal line, untouched. Very flashy, but illegal. The puck comes back and the face-off is inside your own defense zone.

There is an exception here also: you will *not* be called for icing when your team is playing shorthanded due to one or more players sitting in the penalty box for rule infractions.

By now you may have the impression that ice hockey is not for the boy whose hide or spirit bruises easily. Puck and ice are hard, skates are sharp, and a flailing stick can become a damaging weapon. In fact, the game would be too rough for anyone without protective clothing. So you wear heavy gloves, thin in the palms to ensure a good grip and solid control of the stick, but well padded in the fingers and back to prevent injuries. In addition, you wear elbow pads and shin protectors, ankle guards and shoulder pads, knee protectors and padded pants. For proper security you wear a supporter with a plastic cup. Young players are required to wear a helmet with a mouth guard. Many older pros have started wearing helmets and may soon admit to the common sense of adding a mouth guard.

By the time you put all of this safety equipment on your head or under your club socks, shorty pants, and numbered shirt, you weigh about twelve pounds extra. Yet, every ounce is designed to improve your game and protect you from injury.

The cost of the uniform and gear can easily reach $100, although it can be considerably less. The pros spend several times this sum.

With all of the protection, you might think you are as safe from harm as a Sherman tank. But don't be drawn off guard! Plenty of painful things can still happen out on the ice. Accidents, like losing your footing and crashing to the hard, frozen surface. Or not-so-accidental mishaps, like being held, elbowed, kneed, tripped or charged into. Or being slashed, jabbed, boarded, hooked, speared, cross-checked, or hit with a high stick.

20   *Opposite:* View of inner protective gear

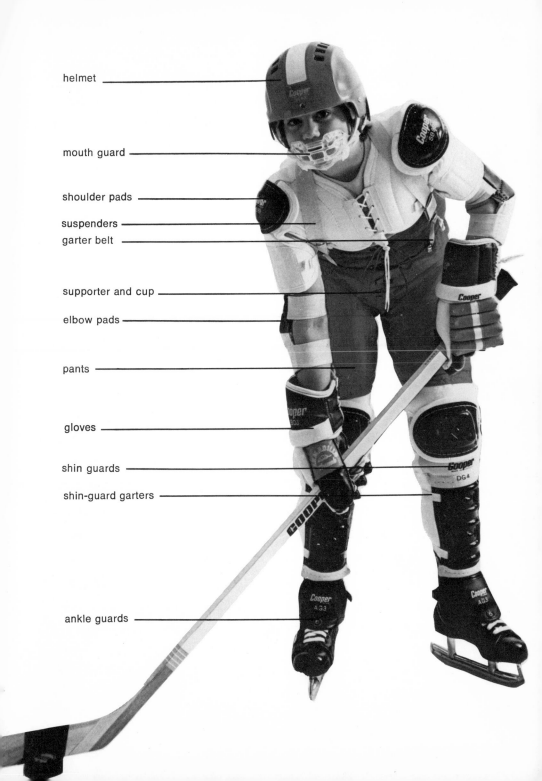

helmet

mouth guard

shoulder pads

suspenders

garter belt

supporter and cup

elbow pads

pants

gloves

shin guards

shin-guard garters

ankle guards

In the case of fouls, somebody has to pay. Officials send the guilty person to the penalty box, leaving his team to carry on shorthanded for a couple of minutes or more.

The game is filled with action and counteraction. One moment you are on the attack, headed for the opponent's goal. But the next moment, an enemy stick pokes in from the side and steals the puck. You reverse your role in midstride. Now you become the attacked and must immediately switch to the defense.

Up the ice, down the ice, chasing, dodging, being chased. You drop to your knees to block a shot. You spring back up and put a hard shoulder check into an opposing wingman. You reach out and get the puck on the end of your stick again, only to have it taken away as someone rides you roughly into the boards.

The action is so fast that free substitution is permitted. In this way fresh players can quickly and smoothly replace those close to dropping from fatigue. And they make the change on the fly, without having to report to an official or without stopping play. Hockey is one of the few games that does not allow time-outs. The only other chances you have to grab a breath are when the whistle blows the puck dead for a face-off or during the fifteen-minute intermissions between the three twenty-minute periods that make a game.

You do not have to be a superman to find fun in ice hockey, but you must like to compete in fast, clashing action, be aggressive, and be physically hard. Toughen your muscles through exercises—torso twists, plenty of push-ups, deep knee bends, and sit-ups. Run a lot. Get your wind in good order. Once in shape, keep up the exercises. They will help to prevent those minor injuries and pulled muscles that are sometimes induced by the quick stops and changes in direction that are required of the player.

If, all in all, you are in good physical condition, willing to practice hard, learn the skills, and take a few spills, then playing ice hockey can be one of the great joys and challenges of your life.

chapter two
SKATING

As you dodge and weave down the ice, your head must be up and your eyes alert to what is going on all around you. Skating must be as easy for you as walking.

So the most important part of ice hockey is simply the ability to skate well. You must be able to skate forward and backward, to circle or move sideways— fast or slow on any kind of ice—automatically without looking down at your skates.

Choose your skates with great care, for cheap skates will not give firm ankle and tendon support nor will

24

they stay sharp. Neither the skates nor the shoes to which they are attached will hold up under the hard usage that they will receive. You do not need a $90 pair of professional skates, but a sturdy pair of well-booted blades still will run anywhere from $20 to $40, depending upon size and quality. So shop around to get the best for your money.

A common mistake is buying skates several sizes too big so that a young player will not outgrow them right away. Filling them up with extra pairs of socks will not provide the firm support of close-fitting skates. So it is

Hockey blades are short with the ends upcurved to aid maneuvering.

unwise to buy them more than a half-size bigger than your street shoes. In fact, the pros often wear skates a half-size *smaller* than their street shoes. But if your feet are still growing, the short time you would be able to wear such skates might put a serious strain on the budget.

Hockey blades are special. Only a few inches of steel lie flat on the ice. The two ends curve upward in what is called the "radius." A blade with a radius is better than a flat blade such as goalies wear, for it permits twisting, turning, dodging, and reversing direction. Yet, you do need enough flat steel on the ice to give you speed and steadiness. Skillful grinding can change the radius of a blade. Many players experiment until they have just the right curve, called "rockering," for their kind of skating.

A defenseman likes a little more blade on the ice to support his body checks and back up the more solid type of skating that he does, as compared to the lighter, more agile skating of the speedier forwards.

Skating in ice hockey is strictly stop-and-go. On rare occasions you can break away for a burst of speed down the rink. But most of the action consists in darting in one direction, slamming on the brakes, reversing

26

yourself quickly, circling tightly, and spurting off on another tack. You do need speed, but mostly in spurts.

Even more important than speed are balance and control, for someone is always trying to knock you off your feet. Try to be as solid as a rock, from the ice up. Don't let your ankles turn outward on the blades. Good skate shoes have proper ankle supports and wraparound tendon guards. Lace your skates taut, but not so tight as to hinder circulation. A good fit and firm lacing give the feeling that foot and skate are a single, well-controlled unit.

Skating should be automatic, under full body control.

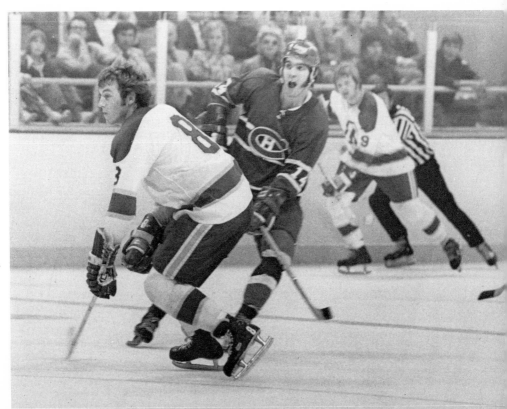

After you are laced up and ready, you begin to work on control and balance by skating, skating, and skating some more. Long hours on blades, keeping your ankles straight and your blade edges firmly on the ice, is the only way to prevent wobbly, shaky, unsure skating.

But you don't skate only with your feet. Skating demands *complete* body control. As you push off hard with the inside edge of your rear skate, bend your

Once you have the puck under control . . .

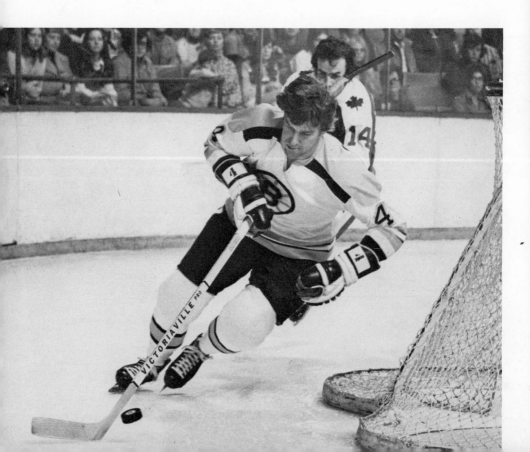

knees slightly and lean forward to maintain good balance. Keep your shoulders level and out ahead of your hips a little, leaning in the direction of travel.

Keep your head up so you are able to see trouble coming. Being forewarned, in most cases you can dodge away from it. Also you will maintain better body posture. Your chest is not pinched, and you are able to breathe deeply. In the rigorous game of hockey you need all of the oxygen you can get.

. . . keep your head up and plan your attack.

Another method for getting under way quickly is to take a few short running steps on your toes, then swing into the push-and-glide motion that provides good momentum. Take long strides, shortening them as emergencies occur. If you keep your blades close to the ice, you will scarcely feel them contacting the surface at the beginning of each stride. Lifting blades high is wasted motion and bogs down your ability to change speed and direction. But opponents like high-steppers —they love to dump them while a blade is high off the surface.

Skate with a rhythmic swinging of your arms. The fact that you are carrying a stick need not spoil that rhythm. Actually the stick should be made a part of it as you pump along, one skate forward, opposite shoulder back, swinging shoulders and stick in a smoothly repeating cadence.

Stopping is as important as starting. The quickest and surest way to brake your momentum is to dig one or both blades into the ice at a ninety-degree angle to your direction of travel. This maneuver is called a "hockey stop."

In a single-leg stop, lift one skate and turn your body sideways in the direction of that skate. Leaning to the rear, dig the inside edge of the forward skate into the ice. As you grate to a stop in a cloud of ice shavings, your uplifted skate is already on its way down, pointed in whatever direction you want to go. You shove off hard with the skate you have used for braking. With the single-leg stop, there is no pause in motion. Of course, you should practice this stop from both right and left sides.

In a double-leg stop, you twist your body and skates quickly to either side, at the same time throwing your weight to the rear and straightening your knees as you dig in with both blades. The double-leg stop offers twice the braking power, is simpler to perform, and probably will be your most effective way to come to a quick halt.

After you have scratched to an ice-shaving stop, you will normally get back into action by making a little jump to get your skates pointed in the right direction. A couple of short running steps to build up momentum, and you are back in your full skating stride.

Most dramatic of the double-leg stops is the jump stop. For a quick halt, you take a little jump, turn sideways in midair, and hit the ice on both blades. But you will need to have good ankles and know what you're doing, for the jump stop takes great skill and practice. A slight error will send you crashing to the ice and skidding off across the rink out of the play.

If you've got time, you may brake simply by dragging your rear skate on the ice at a right angle to the direction of your path. In the heat of action, however, you will normally use one of the other more positive methods of braking.

The art of skating includes mastering many little

A double-leg stop

skills. Learn to use a crossover step, with each leg alternately crossing over the other as you cut a fast corner in an end zone. This is the same step that speed skaters use on turns. But an ice-hockey rink is cramped, so you keep your strides shorter. Work on this technique, for the crossover step is speed skating at its finest.

Quick starts and instant stops, all kinds of turns and pivots, plus the ability to skate backwards almost as well as forward are the skills you must acquire if you take your hockey seriously. You will quickly realize that you must practice everything in both directions. By doing figure eights, you'll soon become as adept at left-hand turns as at right-hand turns. Do wind sprints forward and backward from one end of the rink to the other to build stamina. Practice different braking methods. Keep drilling until you are as at home on that pair of thin hollow-ground blades as a goat on a mountain.

You will soon learn, if you don't know by now, that you can play hockey only as well as you can skate.

chapter three
QUICK WITH THE STICK

Once you have mastered skating, it is time to get busy with your stickhandling. The two, of course, go together like squirrels and acorns.

To be a good stick handler, you must first choose the right stick for you. Usually made of ash, today's hockey sticks are often reinforced with fiber glass, particularly in and around the blade. The fiber glass strengthens the blade and the area where it joins the ash handle and also protects the stick from moisture.

According to rules, the stick can be no more than fifty-five inches long from the heel of the blade to the tip of the shaft. The pros use a stick about fifty-three inches long.

A precise length at the beginning is not so important. You can always trim a little off a shaft that proves too long. After cutting, you can simply tape the end or add a butt knob under the tape for better gripping.

Perhaps the best way to pick a stick that fits you is to stand in your street shoes and hold the stick so it rests on the tip of its blade. The end of the shaft should reach your mouth. If you're on skates when measuring, the butt of the stick should reach your chin. This method is one commonly used, but trial and error probably is the only sure way to determine which stick is just right for you.

Pick a stick of a decent weight. It should not be so heavy that you can't manage it easily or so light that you are unable to ward off the stick attacks of your opponents. A little whip to the shaft will help control the puck. Too much whip shows weakness, and the stick may break during a slap shot or in a melee around the goal mouth.

The lie of a stick, which is the angle of the blade to the shaft, is very important. Lies are numbered for convenience, from about 3 to 8. The lower the number, say 3 or 4, the flatter or more open is the angle of the blade to the stick shaft. Players who crouch low as they handle the puck, or who rag the puck out away from them, prefer the low lies. Players who skate more

Pick the lie that is most comfortable for you.
Inset: Typical hockey-stick lies.

upright and like to keep the puck in close may use a stick with a higher lie, say a 7 or 8. By and large, the medium 5 or 6 lie is favored by most players.

Picking the right lie is a matter of comfort. Where do you prefer to work the puck? Close in or out a ways? Are you inclined to skate fairly erect or in a crouch? What comes most naturally to you? Where does the puck feel right? When you find at least partial answers to these questions, pick a stick with the lie that puts the bottom of the blade flat on the ice where you want it. This is all-important, for a cardinal rule of stickhandling is to keep that blade on the ice as much as possible in order to control the puck or receive a pass.

Stick blades can be no longer than twelve and a half inches. The width of the blade can be between two and three inches. (These dimensions do not apply to the goalie's stick, which is entirely different.) Today most stick blades have a curve in them, and they are commonly called "banana blades." The curve helps to control the puck when you shoot, pass, or receive on your forehand side. But this steals a little control from your backhand, for you are handling the puck on the outward curve of the blade.

A "banana blade" forms a curved pocket for the puck.

However, the disadvantage is slight, and the curved blade is almost universally favored. Regulations limit the curve to not more than a one-half inch hollow measured from a straight line drawn from any point on the heel to the tip of the blade.

Tape is very much a part of an ice-hockey stick. Plain black friction tape is most commonly used. Adhesive tape and other tapes of various colors and textures also are used. The tape should be rough in texture to provide grip on the puck.

Taping the blade definitely helps to control the puck, whether shooting, passing, or simply ragging it down the ice. The tape should be changed after a game so the moisture that is trapped underneath will dry. Moisture will soften and ruin a blade. Don't tape too heavily. A single overlapping layer is enough. And it is better not to tape the entire blade. Tape only the center part, perhaps half of the blade, that gets most of the action.

Taping all or part of the stick shaft is strictly a matter of personal preference. Do whatever might improve your grip.

Holding a hockey stick properly is an art in itself. A poorly held stick, or a grip that lacks natural comfort, will weaken your ability to control the stick fully.

If someone held a broom out to you, with which hand would you reach for it? Usually it is your stronger hand, your right hand if you are right-handed. No doubt this is the way you would reach for a hockey stick.

You would then grip the stick lower down on the shaft with your other hand—in this case the left hand —your stick-pushing hand. Your natural forehand shot would thus be made from the left side, and in hockey terms this makes you a left-handed shooter. If the right hand is the low one on the stick and the normal forehand shot is made from the right side, you are a right-handed shooter.

Although the lower hand on the stick shaft provides the main power to a pass or a shot, your stronger hand should be on top. At times that hand alone will carry and control the stick.

In holding the stick, you will normally grip it with the top hand hooked over the upper edge of the shaft so that the back of the fist is away from your body. The lower hand, twelve or so inches down the stick, grips the shaft from underneath, with the knuckles toward you. Thus the hands take opposite positions. This permits a sort of scissoring action—top hand pulling back, bottom hand thrusting forward—when snapping a pass. The same applies when taking a shot, except that usually you lower your bottom hand farther down on the shaft for added leverage.

The prime concern in choosing a grip is to settle

A left-handed shooter   A right-handed shooter

on one that is most comfortable and gives you the best control. Don't worry whether it turns out to be right- or left-handed.

Just as you don't look at your skates, you don't watch your stick as you work the puck down the ice. Your head should be up in order for you to see to pass,

41

One-handed stick control often enables
a quick breakaway up ice.

know what you are doing, and to be able to avoid the
stick checks and body bumps of opponents.

Stickhandling the puck, therefore, is done mostly by
feel. In ragging the puck down the ice, you nudge it
gently from the front of your stick to the back. The

slight pressure each time your stick comes in contact with the disc will tell you whether or not you have control. Naturally you can glance at the puck now and then to be sure everything is all right. But primarily your eyes are up, planning your route, preparing your moves, and looking for teammates.

With practice you will learn not to tap the puck so hard that it skids beyond the reach of your stick. On the other hand, you must not tap it so lightly that you overskate it. In either case you have lost stick control. Nudging the puck gently is best. In fact, some players are known to practice with eggs or tennis balls in order to develop the right touch—feather-light, yet in full control.

When stickhandling the puck down the ice, try to keep it on the side away from an attacking opponent. This will enable you to avoid poke checks and the like. To do so you must be able to control the puck on both sides of your blade, and to stickhandle from both forehand and backhand sides—the same kind of versatility demanded in your basic skating.

While gripping the stick with your strong top hand, you sometimes take your lower hand off the shaft and carry the puck out ahead of you with one-handed stick-

The stick handler must be able to feint, pivot,
twist, or somehow get past the defenseman.

work. This is done primarily on a breakaway down
the ice, when the whole purpose is to streak out ahead
of your opponents.

With a good one-handed grip on your stick, when
you don't have the puck, you can reach far out and
check or sweep the puck away from your opponent.
Or better still, scoop it up and steal it away.

But remember that you can easily lose control of a stick held by only one hand, or it can be whacked out of your grasp.

While stickhandling, twist your stick a quarter turn forward to put the full blade flat on the ice. The angle also cups the blade slightly over the puck, forming something of a pocket in which you can keep the puck under firm control. Cup and release the puck from one side of the stick to the other repeatedly as you move down the ice. And do so as automatically as you blink your eyes.

Only stickwork scores in hockey. A good player must be a good stick handler.

chapter four
PASSING

A winning team is invariably a good passing team. A passing attack is the best way to storm an opponent's goal. A passing team will bewilder and outmaneuver a team weak in passing. But a good passing game is not a matter of wild and lucky puck action. A team that passes its opponent silly is one made up of six guys who have mastered moving the puck so skillfully that they perform without having to think.

Back of such a performance lie many hours of passing practice. Effective passing starts with the grip. Grip the stick shaft firmly, but don't squeeze it. Don't grasp it deeply in the palm; control it more with your fingers. When you are in full control, the stick will be like an extension of your arm. You won't need to watch it in order for it to do its job.

Pass crisply. Keep your stick blade on or close to the ice. This is an important habit to develop whether you are passing, receiving, shooting, or stickhandling. A high blade causes more misses and errors than any other single aspect of puck handling.

Pick your target, then make your pass.

You must, of course, be careful not to pass too far forward and be called for offside. Move the puck zone by zone. Not only do rules require short passes, but they are more accurate and are less subject to costly interceptions.

Avoid passing backwards when possible. You should always try to pass the puck forward up the ice to a teammate nearer to the opponent's goal. In hockey this is called "headmanning."

The sweep, or flat, pass is commonly used when the ice around you is not unduly crowded. The idea of a sweep pass is to keep the puck low and easy for a teammate to receive. To perform it, tip your blade slightly over the puck to insure control and hold it on the ice. Then start the pass with the puck near the middle of your blade, sweeping the stick forward and rolling the puck off the toe of the blade.

Avoid slapping the puck when you make a pass. Not only is slapping much less accurate, but it may set the puck rolling or tumbling over the ice, making it tough to receive.

However you pass, judge properly and aim well ahead of the receiver, yet not too far ahead or he won't be able to reach the puck. On the other hand, if you give him too small a lead, he will have to break stride or reach back for it.

The artistry of a proper pass lies in putting the puck right onto the receiver's stick without his having to alter his speed or break his rhythm.

As the pass leaves your stick, *follow through*. This after motion will ensure both speed and accuracy. With the pass on its way, your stick shaft should end up pointing toward the receiver.

A sweep pass right between a defenseman's skates

During a scramble on the ice, you don't often have time to go through the smooth, deliberate motions of a good sweep pass. When you get hold of a puck you'll seldom be able to keep it for more than a moment. In that moment, you must pick your receiver, judge your lead, and hit him with a quickly released wrist pass.

The wrist pass, also known as a snap or push pass, is less accurate than the sweep pass, but it does get the puck out of the mix-up and, with luck, to a teammate. This pass is propelled by a quick scissoring of the wrists, rather than a full arm-and-shoulder movement. The passer should follow through as well as crowded quarters will allow, for the follow-through is often the difference between getting the puck to its target or having it go wild.

A flip pass is another effective way to move the puck up the rink. It is like a chip shot in golf and is used to loft the puck over an opponent's reaching stick or outthrust skate, or even over his prone body. It lifts the puck *over* obstacles, instead of trying to zing through them.

But the flip pass requires delicate stick control. You must get the edge of the blade on the *bottom* edge of the puck, then twist your wrists to flip the puck into the air. You must, of course, have the stick snapping forward in order to give speed and direction to the pass.

A receiver may have trouble taking control of a flip pass. The puck often bounces and rolls erratically when it hits the ice. Still the pass is good for getting the puck free of sticks and out of a tangle. It should

Look at the target and follow through with the stick across your body.

be practiced regularly and used when clearly needed.

A drop pass is a tricky move that only a well-disciplined team can employ without blundering. Let's say you are skating up the ice ahead of your teammates, ragging the puck and doing a nice job of stickhandling. Suddenly you are face-to-face with one or more burly defensemen blocking your path to the goal. You're trapped. But a stick slaps the ice behind you, or a familiar voice yelps over your shoulder, "Drop it!"

He's calling for a drop pass. You fake a shot at the goal and quickly stop the puck with the back of your blade. Then, as you continue skating, you leave the puck lying dead on the ice. As you split the defense, or otherwise ride them off the puck, your trailing teammate picks up the little black disc and stickhandles it goalward. Or, if he's close enough, he takes a shot at the net, perhaps aided by your screening the goalie's view of the puck.

The drop pass is a gamble. You don't have time to see who is slapping his stick behind you or calling for the puck. So your team must have a foolproof set of signals in order to prevent an opponent from tricking your players into handing him a free drop pass.

A variation of the drop pass is the back pass. It is executed in the same way, except that you push the puck rearward off your blade, instead of merely leaving it dead on the ice.

There are other useful passes for special situations. The carom pass, used to ricochet the puck off the boards, is a handy way to outwit opponents. Your checker moves in on you. You bank your pass against

Backhanding a pass

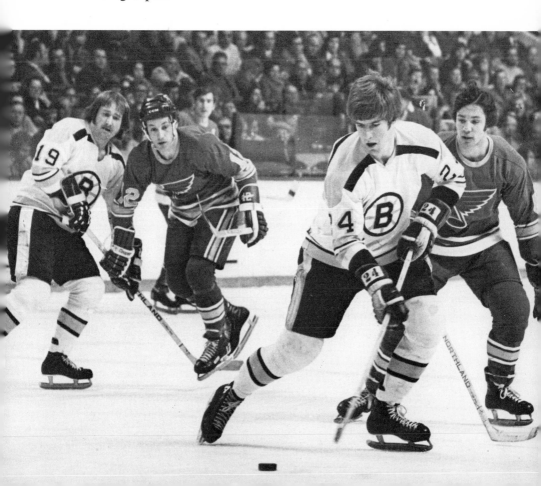

Passing away from the boards.

the boards to a teammate. Or, in fact, you skate
around the checker, pick up your own banked pass,
and go on your way. (Before each game you should
test the liveliness of the rink boards so you will have a
good idea of how the puck will bounce.)

You also should be adept at passing the rubber disc
around the curved corners. Often this is a better way
to get the puck to a teammate on the far side of the
rink than trying to pass across the ice. Around-the-

Pulling the stick through on a back pass

corner passes in the defense zone also avoid the hazardous mistake of passing in front of your own goal.

Deflection passes also are important to good teamwork. Players should practice deflecting passes off their own stick to a third teammate. This is a fast way of moving the puck around and confounding the opposition.

All passes can be made off the backhand as well as the forehand side, and during passing drills you should pay equal attention to both sides. If an opponent senses you have a weak backhand, he will know just how to play you, and you will be only half the threat you might have been. So practice those backhand passes.

Always remember that your pass is a good one only if your receiver is able to control it. Don't send him a bullet when he is only five feet away—it will be gone before he gets his stick on it. On the other hand, if your receiver is across the rink, you'd better put plenty of mustard on the pass to keep it from being snared by an enemy stick.

Firing the puck is only half of a pass. The other half is receiving it. A quarterback can win football games simply by putting the ball in the air. But hockey players can't specialize—they've got to be able to receive as well as to pass. If you obey the basic rule of hockey and keep your stick blade close to the ice, you at least have the correct start. That is the only way you will always be ready to receive a pass, which you may or may not have expected. Letting the puck get away from you under your stick blade is inexcusable. Few things do more to make a coach shake his head in despair.

In fact, you must get the entire blade on the ice in order to have the largest possible receiving area facing the puck. Be sure to turn the blade at a right angle to the path of the approaching disc. Then the puck will hit squarely against the surface and not glance off at a tangent and skitter out of reach. The closer to the middle of the blade that you receive the puck, the better control you will have over it. Again, when catching the puck, tip the blade slightly forward and over it to form a slight pocket or trap.

Catch a pass squarely, with stick on the ice
and the blade cupped slightly over it.

When receiving, don't meet the pass with a hard stick. Let your stick give a little as the puck reaches it. In this way you soften the contact and keep the disc from bounding away.

Unfortunately, all passes that come your way will not approach at exactly the right speed or be in the right place, for hockey is not that precise a sport. You must do whatever is called for in order to gain control of the skidding disc. When the passer has not led you properly, you will be out ahead of the puck's path. You must slow down or even reach back to get it. It is perfectly legal to stop the puck with your skates. Many a good player gets skillful at this maneuver. Not only does he stop the puck, but while still speeding across the slippery ice, he kicks it out ahead where he can get stick control of it.

On the other hand, the passer may lead you too much, and you can't reach the puck. You may have to bend low or go down on one knee, thrusting your stick far out and flat on the ice as you try to hook it or somehow stop it.

You can take your eyes off the puck once you get full control of it. Handle it by feel. Watch what's going on around you, and plan your next move.

Put as much practice into passing and receiving as into shooting and skating. Each depends fully upon the other. Keep in mind that you can move the puck forward quicker with a pass than by stickhandling it down the ice. Always watch for the man breaking out ahead of you. Be ready to zip a pass over to him. Then streak out ahead and get ready to receive a return pass.

Practice passes with your teammates. Long passes, short passes, sweep, wrist, flip, and drop passes. Arrow some of them across the ice. But take a lot of the zip out of others, for accuracy more than speed is the mark of a good pass.

There are no rules to tell you just how far, how hard, or when to pass. Only practice and game experience will teach you the difference between good passing and bad passing, which usually is the difference between winning and losing.

chapter five

SHOT ON GOAL

One of the most thrilling and challenging moments in any hockey game begins when you snake the puck out of a tangle of players. You cradle the disc on the end of your stick, dig in your skates, and start up the ice ahead of the pack. Such a breakaway is rare in a closely fought game. A good defense prevents it.

But if you are lucky enough to make such a breakaway, as you cross the blue line into the attacking zone, you will focus your attention on the goalie. What is he going to do? How are you going to get that puck past him and into the net?

60

This is what the game is all about—getting in close and taking a shot on goal!

Although you will do anything legal to get that puck into the net, there are three basic shots you can use. The most common is the wrist shot, which is not unlike a wrist pass, but even faster and more powerful. You start the wrist shot when the puck is a little behind the plane of your body. This cocks your wrists and allows a full forward movement of the stick.

You begin the forward motion with the stick blade

A rare breakaway brings about a quick showdown between shooter and goalie.

tipped slightly over the puck in order to keep it in full control. But, unlike a pass, where you try to keep the puck on the ice, your best wrist shot lifts the puck into one of the corners of the goal. You aim it either high or low, depending upon the goalie's position or his weakness, if any.

So, just as you release the puck with a snap of your wrists, you tilt the blade back a little to give the disc an upward trajectory. Having already picked your target, you keep your eyes on it. As the puck starts its flight, you follow through with your stick.

The most vulnerable spot for most goalies is low and on the stick side. In the high corner on the stick side is another good spot. Even if the goalie is able to block the shot with his stick, skates, or pads, he does not usually get full control of it. The puck may ricochet into the net. You can't count on it, though. So you or one of your teammates must follow in and be ready to tap a rebound through the crease.

It is much harder to pass a goaltender on his glove side. He can move his glove a lot faster than his stick. And, like a good first baseman, he snags the puck in his webbing and drops it off to one of his teammates or freezes it for a face-off.

62

So you start the wrist shot with the puck near your trailing foot and away from your body. You drive off your back skate. As you sweep the puck forward, you shift the weight to your front skate, snapping the puck off the tip of your blade. You follow through, with wrists, arms, shoulders, and back all adding power to the shot.

The second basic shot, used more at close range than far out, is the flip shot. Like the flip pass, it is intended to lift the puck over obstacles such as a fallen

Shooting high on the goalie's stick side
is a good way to score.

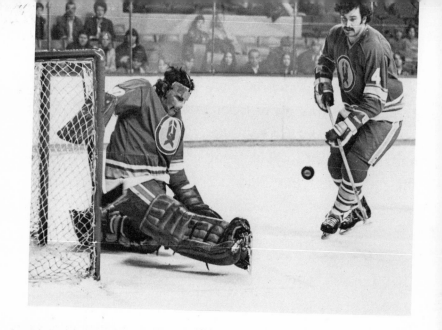

Looping a flip shot over a goalie's outstretched leg.

goalie or to loop it over a defenseman's sweep check.

Power is not the object of a flip shot. In fact, a soft flip shot is most effective in near the goal mouth. While everyone is scrambling and whacking sticks to get possession of the puck, you reach in, get the bottom of your blade under the edge of the puck, flip your wrists, and loop it into the net.

Some players try flip shots from way out near the blue line. Since a flip shot rolls or bounces erratically across the ice, occasionally one will get past the goalie. But not often. The most you can hope from a long flip shot is to put the puck in the vicinity of the enemy goal, so a teammate can tip it on in.

Both wrist and flip shots can be made from the backhand side. The grip remains the same as for a forehand shot, but the action is reversed, with the lower hand pulling the stick instead of pushing it.

Backhand shots are most effective and score many goals from close in, one reason being that such a shot

Having deked the goalie out of position, the shooter tries to sneak in a backhand shot.

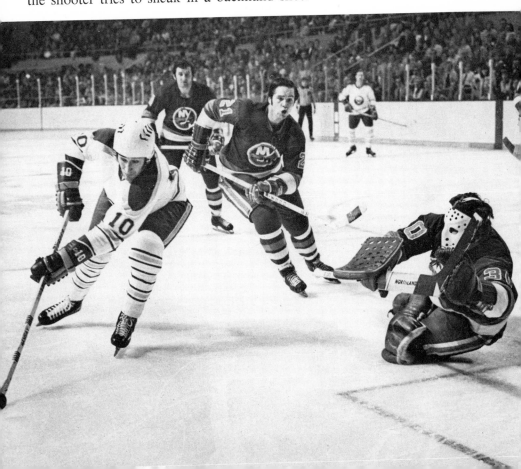

often takes a goalie by surprise. As you charge toward the net, the goalie follows your every motion. He waits for you to make the first move so he can counter it. He may come out several yards from the goal mouth to meet you. This tactic narrows the angle at which you can shoot the puck past him. Your chances get slimmer by the moment.

To counter his moves, you may "deke" him—fake the shot off your forehand. He lunges to block the path. But instead of going through with the shot, you stop the puck with the back of your blade and pivot to the opposite side away from the goalie's ready defense. Then, with the puck still nestling on the back of your stick blade, you slip it past the goaltender and into the net. By adding a little tilt to the backhand swinging blade, you simply flip the puck into one of the upper corners of the net.

Above all, don't be a one-way shooter. Practice both forehand and backhand shots regularly. You may not develop equal strength on both sides, but at least you will avoid having a backhand weakness that an opponent can and will take quick advantage of.

The third basic shot in hockey is the slap shot. It is the most dramatic, the most energetic, and by far the

66

loudest shot in hockey. Though less accurate than some of the more controlled shots, it is action-packed and favored by the spectators.

There is nothing subtle about a slap shot. The delighted fans see you haul back your stick, swing it forward with all or most of your might, and crash it into the puck at the bottom of the arc. The fans assume that you then cross your fingers and hope somehow you manage to blast the disc past the goalie.

The slap shot

But the slap shot is not so carelessly done as that. Like everything else in hockey, it demands precision and a definite sequence of unfolding action.

Let's look at a typical slap shot.

You're going to shoot from the left side. That is, your left hand is low on the stick shaft, but now you lower it a couple of inches more for greater power. (It also helps prevent your stick from breaking, which is a risk of a vigorous slap shot.) You keep your controlling hand on the end of the stick just as you do in other stickhandling plays.

Then, as you approach the puck, either dead on the ice or still moving, you start your backswing with the puck a couple of feet off your forward skate. Don't overdo the backswing by bringing the stick way up behind and above your head. The defenders may not give you all the time in the world to complete it. Besides, if you hold your backswing to about shoulder height, you have ample arc to put plenty of power into your forward swing.

Extend your lower hand away from your body. Keep it straight in order to get a full swing. Your right hand, gripping the top of the shaft, should also be out away from your body.

Starting the swing with weight on your trailing foot, you lean into the puck. Your low hand powers the stick forward, while your upper hand levers back the butt of the stick. Again, it is a scissoring motion. As the stick blade arches down, you shift your weight to the other skate as it comes striding forward.

At the bottom of the arc bring your blade against the ice a scant inch behind the puck. In almost the same instant the stick cracks against the rubber disc.

You must hit the puck in the center of the blade or toward the heel. By hitting it forward of center, the force of contact will twist the blade and make your shot go awry.

As contact is made, give a little extra wrist action to your lower hand to lift the puck off the ice. How much twist depends upon how high a target you pick. You also tighten your grip, hoping to keep the blade steady even if you have hit the puck a little off-center on your blade.

By now your rear skate is off the ice, and you are well into the all-important follow-through.

The slap shot is a power shot, often attempted from far out. It is widely used by defensemen as they hover near the blue line or even back near the red center line, which limits the length of any legal shot. The slap shot is feared by goalies, for it may come in at over 100 miles per hour! What it lacks in accuracy, it makes up for in sheer overpowering speed.

The best distance to attempt a shot on goal is about ten to fifteen feet away from the goalie, close enough for accuracy, yet far enough out so that you can pick a juicy target in the four-by-six-foot goal mouth.

If you can approach from the dead center, known as the "slot," you will have the widest target for a shot. But you can expect the defense to try to crowd you toward the sides. The target narrows in proportion to their success in checking you toward the boards on either side. The narrower the angle becomes, the better the goalie's chance of protecting his cage. So don't wait too long, or try to get in too close before shooting. Any good defensive team will ride you off toward the boards, and your chance of getting a straight-on shot at goal will disappear.

Look for the goalie's weakness as you bear down on him. Are his legs apart? Shoot for the opening. Does he hug one side of the net more than the other? Work for a shot at the wider side. Is he better with his stick hand than his glove hand? Go for the weak side.

Does he have the habit of flopping in front of a shot? Shoot high.

To become a sharpshooting scorer you must drill and practice goal shots. But don't be greedy—never shoot when you can pass to a teammate in a better position for a shot on goal. Assist his effort with a well-placed pass. As a matter of fact, in ice hockey the assist is as important as the shot and is rated equal to it in individual scoring records.

Be a good shooter, therefore, but don't hog the puck. And who knows? Someday you may put that biscuit in the basket three times during a game, thereby doing the hat trick.

The important follow-through

chapter six
ON OFFENSE

Ice hockey records show that in nearly three quarters of the games the team that scores first wins. This stands to reason, for the team with the stronger offense usually gets the jump on the other team.

In ice hockey, your offense begins the moment the first puck is dropped onto the ice. If you take possession of it at the opening face-off, you serve warning that you are out to win, which may put your opponent in a defensive mood. And that is just what you want.

Whether in the face-off or later, you usually must be able and willing to meet strength with strength to get

72

that puck. This does not mean being overly rough or unsportsmanlike. During a game you will be reminded often that ice hockey is a contact sport. You will be reminded each time an opponent shoulder checks you hard into the boards, each time a solid hip sends you spinning across the ice or a stick cracks against your shins. You'll soon realize that to play hockey you need a sound body, a stout heart—and guts.

You must be able to take your lumps as well as dish them out. If you let an opponent bluff or intimidate you, your game will fall apart. Establish your rights and protect your position on the team. Even if your opponent is bigger, a good, hard-driving body check

Hockey begins with the face-off.

will separate him from the puck, and he will regard you with respect and caution.

Self-confidence is the key. Know you are a winner, and play like one—aggressively.

There are no one-way players in ice hockey. At one moment you and your teammates have the puck. Your fire is up. You charge down the ice, snapping passes, heading for an almost sure goal. Then something goes wrong. A pass skids wide, or a defenseman reaches in front of you and pokes the puck away.

In a split second, and in midstride, you must switch roles. You are no longer being chased as you threaten to score. You are now the chaser, on defense, trying desperately to prevent being scored upon.

Hockey demands that a player be adept at both offensive and defensive play. You must be the master of more skills than players of most other sports.

The main offensive thrust in an ice-hockey game is carried by the line, or forwards, made up of the center, plus the left and right wingmen. These three usually take the attack into the enemy zone.

Such a three-man line is made up of players who practice together until they know all of each other's

Ice hockey is a game of lumps—you must be able to
take them as well as give them.

moves and, thus, are able to play as a unit. A good line
is hard to break up. When substitutions are made,
often on the fly, usually the entire three-man line
hurdles the boards and hits the ice together, as the
other line leaves the game for a breather.

Because of the exhausting nature of ice hockey and
the freqent substitution of players, teams always have
at least two lines ready for play, often more. A coach
knows that a line is effective at full pace for only about
a minute and a half. Then he pulls the men out and
sends in a fresh line.

A really effective offense, of course, is made up of all five players. (Naturally the goalie, who stays behind to protect his net, doesn't join in a charge up the ice. In fact, goalies are not allowed to go beyond the center red line.) The defensemen are particularly helpful in getting hold of the puck and starting it forward by headmanning passes to teammates moving up ice. By and large, however, the defensemen trail the attack and let the center and wings make the main rushes on the opponent's goal.

At times, though, a defenseman will seize the opportunity to keep driving goalward. Then it is up to one of the wingmen to drop back and cover for him in case the puck changes hands and the attack switches to the opposite direction. A team must never leave the goalie unprotected.

Because hockey is such a fast and ever-changing game, it cannot be played by a rigid formula. Yet, despite the instant changes of direction and other variables, a game must follow a basic plan.

In simplest terms that means there must be a system of attack, with defensemen and forwards taking part.

If you happen to be playing center, you will probably be the play maker. When your goalie makes a save and clears the puck out to a defenseman, you start up the ice. Crossing the nearest blue line into the neutral zone, you take a brisk pass from the defenseman. You dart a glance at your left wingman up ahead and near the boards. He crosses the center line and skates toward a patch of unoccupied ice. Finding open ice is every offensive player's prime concern.

You lead him the way a hunter leads a duck, aiming your pass for the open patch he will soon reach. Your pass is true. He takes it on the end of his stick, going full out, and crosses the last blue line and into the attacking zone.

Though set plays are often upset,
a hockey game must follow a basic plan.

But an opposing defenseman closes in and rides him toward the boards. Meanwhile, you angle toward the goal. The wingman brakes to a stop against the boards and snaps you a backhand pass.

By now you are only about twenty-five feet from the goal mouth. The goalie comes out to meet you. He looks like a well-padded battleship, looming bigger and bigger in your eyes. The closer he gets the more he blots out the sight of your intended target. Before you know it you can see only a small corner of the opening.

You watch his eyes, searching for a clue, waiting for him to commit himself. You bring your stick back, feinting a slap shot. Now he moves, throwing out a padded leg to block your apparent shot on goal. In the process, he sprawls on the ice, throwing everything he has into the path of your shot.

But you don't finish your shot. You slam on your brakes, stop the puck with your blade, and flick a back pass to one of the wingmen following a dozen feet behind you. He is ready for it, because you have practiced the whole offensive maneuver time and time again.

Before the goalie can pull in his outstretched leg and

If the goalie doesn't stop this one, the player at left
is in good position to deflect the shot into the net.

straighten up, the wingman flips the puck into the un-
defended net. The red light flashes. Your team has
scored.

Were all offensive charges, or even half of them, as
pat and successful as this, hockey would be a simple
game to play. But they seldom are. Any real attack
must take into account the fact that for every move
you make one or more of your opponents will make a
countermove.

That countermove has a single purpose—to separate you from the puck, if not from your senses. So
you learn to slip away from body checks. You must be
a good enough skater to dodge away from a defense-

man bent upon crushing you into the boards. You must be able to feint, stickhandle, pass, and shoot with the best of them.

Since the puck so often ends up in one of the corners, an aggressive team will try to control them. Whenever possible, a player should be handy to pick up hard passes shot directly to a corner. Or the puck may come zipping "around the horn," that is, ricocheting along the boards from the opposite corner.

So game control means corner control. But no worthy opponent will let you have the corners free. You'll have to earn them.

It also is a good plan to have a player on the attacking team hovering around the net whenever possible. He is sometmes called the "garbage man," for he has several important functions. He may screen out the goalie's view of an incoming shot. He may be in position to deflect a wide shot just enough to tip it into the net. Or, as the garbage man, he keeps moving around just waiting to pounce on a rebound from the goalie's pads or stick and dump it quickly into the net.

He must, however, be careful not to get in the way and interfere with a good shot by a teammate.

* * *

Nothing is more important to an offense than winning the draw at the various face-offs during the game, and thereby getting possession of the puck. Success at face-offs depends largely upon being quicker than your opponent. You must anticipate just when and with what force the official will drop the puck. Your stick should be moving before the puck hits the ice. But, of course, so will be your opponent's. You may try to beat him simply by getting your wood on the puck first. Or you may slap his stick with yours, wrecking his rhythm, then sweep the puck aside to a waiting teammate. But you must be fast and powerful. The speed comes from a quick scissoring flick of your wrists.

Usually you try to draw the puck back to your teammates on the defensive side of the face-off circle. And, as in any good frontier tale, the guy with the fastest draw wins.

Hockey is a game of position. Each man usually has his own territory to patrol and protect. You are free to use all parts of the ice, but it is wisest not to bunch up in one place with several members of your team. Not only does this result in crowded and sloppy hockey, but it leaves some other part of the rink un-defended.

Most mistakes in ice hockey occur when the teams are bunched up and everything turns to confusion. So keep the game open. Spread your offense. Work to uncrowded areas where you have room to maneuver. If a teammate swings over into your territory —and this happens often—be ready to slip the puck to him and skate quickly into the gap he has vacated. Such switches help to cross up the defense for a moment.

On offense, the two attacking defensemen usually stick with the play as it moves goalward. But as the action rips across the blue line and into the attacking zone, the defensemen stop their forward rush at the points. These so-called points are the patches of ice just inside the blue line of the attacking zone and a few feet from the boards on each side.

By playing the points, the defensemen are in position to keep the puck in the attacking zone. This is important, for if the puck gets back across the blue line and onto neutral ice, the offense must retreat and reform for a second attack.

The points also form a good safety valve. In case

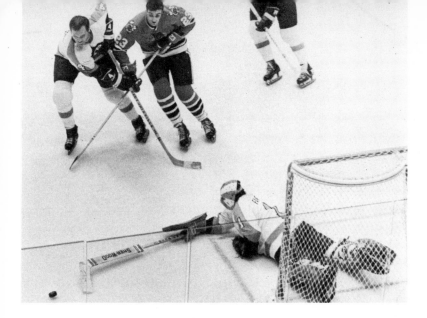

Players duel for a loose puck.

the play used for an attack on goal fails, the puck can be passed back out to one of the point men, who will start a new charge or take a shot on goal.

At the points the defensemen also are in position to intercept most clearing passes made by opposing players trying to flip the puck out of the danger zone.

Your offensive drive depends on your moving constantly and keeping the puck moving. In this way you prevent the defense from digging in. You keep them guessing, which is the only way to get at the goal. And, of course, as you keep moving, keep moving *forward*.

Often an infraction of the rules sends one or even

two members of the opposing team to the penalty box. While they are shorthanded, you have a couple minutes or so to pick up an easy goal.

At least you hope it will be easy, although it never is. When shorthanded, an opposing team sends its finest penalty killers on the ice. These are defensemen whose only job is to prevent you, at all cost, from getting near their goal.

You naturally meet force with force by throwing your best offensive strength against them, clobbering them with your power play. In this maneuver you gang up on the defending team. All five of your players invade the attacking zone, trying to penetrate the weakened defense, which huddles around the goal. To blast through that human barrier, even though you outnumber them, demands power.

You might work the puck in according to a plan. Flip a pass to an unguarded teammate to make your opponents spread out their already thin defense. Shake another player loose. Feint and decoy. Play cat and mouse until one of your teammates is in the slot and free to shoot. Then snap him a pass, and watch him deke the goalie and slip the biscuit in the net.

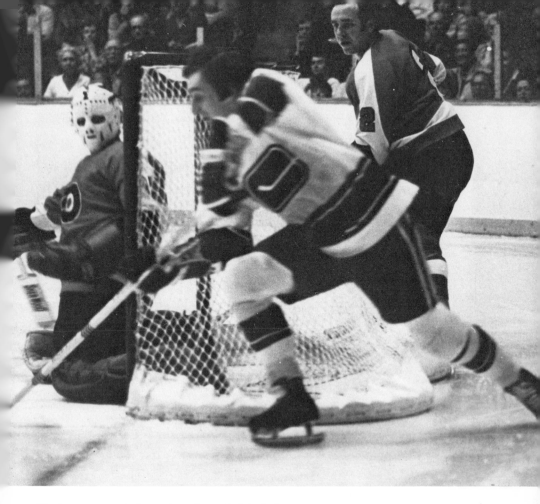

Trying to sneak in a shot from behind the net

While most scores are probably made on planned power plays, sometimes a team may resort to sheer bombardment of the opponent's goal. It figures that if you take enough shots at a weakly defended goal, the puck will eventually find its way into the net. In addition, the fast and furious action is exhausting to the beleagured opponents. Sometimes the barrage tactics work, sometimes not.

Once a team has scored, the opposing team immediately goes back to full strength. Hence, never more than one goal can result from a minor penalty situation.

To sum up, the major things to keep in mind when your team is on the offense is to have a plan: keep the puck moving toward the opponent's goal, keep your stick blade on the ice for both passing and receiving, pass to open ice, watch for rebounds around the enemy goal, and be ready to reverse your direction in a split second.

Never forget, however, that you must be a two-way player. You may be a tiger on offense. But unless you are equally fierce at playing defense, on the scoreboard you will look like a pussycat.

chapter seven
ON DEFENSE

A tough, hard-hitting defense is the backbone of ice hockey. Without a strong defense, you might as well concede defeat.

Each team has two defensemen on the ice. They are your major protection against deep-in attacks. They also are your goalie's best friends, for they see that he is never without protection.

Defensemen usually are the burlier members of a team. As a defenseman, your primary job is to break up plays and grab the puck. This means a lot of body contact, and contact demands muscle and powerful

Forechecking harasses the puck man on his own end of the rink.

skate work. The job of playing defense demands courage.

But a defense does not depend upon the defensemen alone. When you don't have the puck, every member of your team plays defense.

The first thing a forward does when suddenly you lose possession of the puck near your opponent's goal is to begin what is called "forechecking." When you forecheck, you immediately start harassing the other team around their own goal. You poke check, hip check, ride the puck carrier into the boards. You do anything that is legal to hold your opponents back and prevent them from controlling the puck and getting an attack under way. While you are forechecking, the rest of your team is able to organize a more solid defense.

In other words, when you forecheck, you don't fall back and wait for the other team to come to you.

Back-checking begins at mid-ice
and continues into the defending zone.

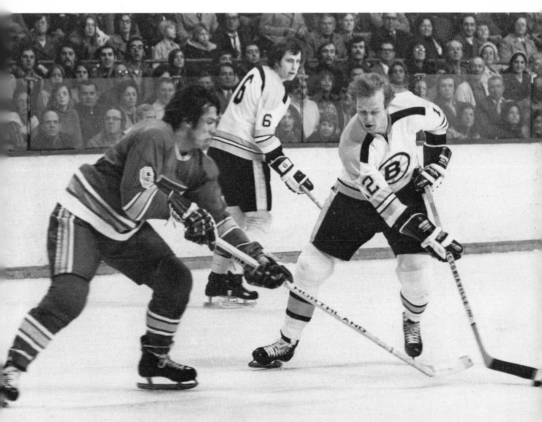

You battle them in their own defending zone, trying to prevent them from breaking out and heading for your goal.

Since forechecking is a temporary action, others of your team must drop back hastily toward your goal. And if the man you are forechecking starts moving up the ice with the puck, you must go with him.

You don't abandon your checking, but as you fall back toward neutral ice and then into your own defense zone, you continue pestering your opponent in what is called "back-checking." The difference between forechecking and back-checking is mainly one of location. In both cases your job is to try to get hold of the puck and, thereby, reverse the action.

There are several ways to force the puck carrier into an error so that you or one of your teammates can steal the puck. They fall into the general category of checks, both body checks and stick checks.

A body check is simply a matter of jarring an opponent in order to make him lose control of the puck. In a shoulder check you drive a shoulder into your man, levering upward for best effect. But your man must have the puck, and you cannot take more than two strides into him.

90

The same is true of a hip check, but a hip check is more of a glancing maneuver. You thrust your hip into your opponent to spoil his timing and perhaps jar him loose from the puck. Properly performed, the hip check leaves you balanced. You brush past, after staggering your opponent, snag the loose puck, and switch the attack.

Body checks are usually made by the defensemen.

Body checking the puck carrier into the boards

A good forward can help by forcing the puck carrier toward the defensemen. Indeed, a good forward often makes his own body checks.

Rather than taking an opponent out of the play by going for his body, it is often better to go directly for the puck. You do so with a variety of stick checks. Try to poke check the puck away by making a one-handed stab at it with your stick. But have a firm grip on the shaft, or you may lose your stick in the scuffle.

Reaching in with a hook check

Or you may try to reach in from behind the skater, or from his blind side, and hook check the puck away from him. The hook check is often a surprise move, for the victim may not realize that you are that close to him. But, again, it takes a long reach and is usually done with the stick held firmly in one hand.

A third commonly used stick check requires you to bend down low, lay your stick almost flat on the ice and sweep it in a wide arc. Often such a sweep check will separate an opponent from the puck.

When you are defending against shots on your goal, you will do anything you can to stop that puck in its goalward flight. Always position yourself between the goal mouth and the puck carrier. If he is able to skate around you, or dodge past you, he's a cinch for at least a shot on goal. And no matter how good a goalkeeper you have, in a one-on-one situation, the shooter has the edge.

So don't let your man get on the goal side of you. When he shoots from far out—and your job is to make him shoot from far out—stop that puck. If you can do so with your stick, or skates, or pads, fine. You may have to drop to your knees and slide toward him to block his shot. Hold your stick out and spread your arms for maximum defense. But be ready and able to spring back up and move in any direction. For the shooter may just be deking you. If you're down on one or both knees and unable to get up quickly, he may feint you out of the play, sprint past you, and be in good position for a shot on goal.

When there seems no other defense against a shot on goal, throw yourself in front of or on the puck! You are not allowed to catch it, although you can bat it down with your hand. Nor are you allowed to

Get the stick down low for a sweep check.

smother it deliberately with your body, although sometimes in the heat of battle the disc does get lodged beneath a player. This situation calls for a face-off.

The main concern, at any cost, is to prevent being scored upon.

The term "at any cost" does, of course, have its limits. Many of the things you might be tempted to do in the wild action of the game are against the rules. If you commit an infraction, you draw a penalty. A minor infraction sits you in the "sin bin" for two

Sometimes you go to a knee drop to stop the puck.

minutes. For more serious infractions, you get five or ten minutes or, indeed, can be ejected from the game.

What's an infraction? Well, you will be penalized if you reach out and hold an opponent by the arm, shirt, or in any other way try to keep him from the puck or out of the play. You cannot elbow him or trip him without drawing a similar penalty.

You may crowd an opponent into the boards, if you are going for the puck, or ride him out of the play. If you body check a man without the puck, you will be called for interference. If you skate more than two strides and slam into him, you will be called for charging. For either infraction, you leave the game for two minutes.

If you do charge, and the official feels that you have fouled deliberately with intent to injure, he will penalize you severely.

Sometimes a hockey stick is mistakenly thought of as a defensive weapon. Of course, in getting possession of the puck the stick is a weapon of sorts. But it is never to be used as such against opposing players. Serious penalties face anyone who does.

If you use your stick as a body hook to reach out and impede an opponent, you are called for hooking.

Hooking with the stick draws a penalty.

Two minutes. Slashing at another player with your stick is another sure way to leave the ice. If injury results, out you go for as long as the officials feel you deserve. In the pro ranks a player is also fined. Nor is spearing a player with the blade of your stick, or even pretending to, permitted. And you won't get away with poking him or ramming him with the end of your stick shaft, called "butt-ending."

High-sticking also is against the rules. Keep your stick below the level of your shoulders. Even then

Spearing a player is not permitted . . .

you are not allowed to grab your stick with two
hands and use it as a battering ram against your opponent. This is known as cross-checking and is yet
another two minutes on the penalty bench.

And, lastly, insofar as sticks are concerned, you
are not allowed to throw your stick for any reason.
To do so draws a major penalty and puts you out of
the game for five minutes.

Should you throw your stick at the puck in a wild
attempt to save what appears to be a sure goal, the

. . . nor is butt-ending.

other team will be awarded a penalty shot at the goal. On a penalty shot the rink is cleared, except for the goalie and one member of the opposing team. And that member is usually their best shooter. In a one-on-one situation, starting with the puck near center ice, the attacking player stickhandles the puck down upon the lonely goalie. Charging in, deking as he comes, the player picks his moment and takes his shot. He gets only one shot, but he succeeds.

Penalty shots are rare. They are a horror to the

Cross-checking is prohibited.

goalie, who probably had nothing to do with the infraction. One way to avoid them is not to throw your stick. If you drop your stick, or it gets knocked out of your hand, simply get hold of it again and go about your game. If you break a stick, you must immediately drop the top end which you still hold and, if possible, kick it toward the boards, away from the action. A jagged stick has no business in the fast action of a hockey game.

When you are backed up to your goal, your first concern, of course, is to block any shots and get possession of the puck. If you succeed on both counts, your next effort should be to clear the puck away from the vicinity of the goal. If you start stickhandling it out, trying to rag the puck away from the goal, you stand a good chance of losing it to a forechecking wingman who is in good position to take a shot.

Pass the puck quickly to the side. That will at least take it out of harm's way for the moment. But don't pass it across the front of your goal where it might be intercepted and shot quickly into the net. Also don't shoot it all the way down to the far end of the rink, or ice it. The puck will be brought back to your end of the rink for a face-off. And you now risk losing it in the face-off.

So clear the puck away from the crease with well-placed passes to teammates breaking free and heading down ice toward the enemy goal.

When your team is beset by penalties, and you are short a player, possibly two (which is the most a team can ever be lacking at one time), you must put your penalty killers on the ice. Their purpose is not to score (although that would be nice if the opportunity popped up). Their job is to eat up the clock for the duration of the penalty. Since your team is outnumbered, those of you still on the ice must pester and harass the opponents in any way you can. Try to keep them off-balance and unable to form a power play. If you get possession of the puck, rag it around or ice it down the rink, which is legal when you are shorthanded. Keep it as far from your defense zone as you can. Above all, try to prevent the other, stronger team from taking it away.

When you are unable to prevent the opposition from moving the puck into the attacking zone, the penalty killers form a box defense around the goal. This formation hinders set plays and forces the opponents to take long shots.

In most defensive situations you should play the man instead of the puck. If you can keep your opponent off-balance or against the boards, or otherwise out of the play, the puck will take care of itself. A teammate will get it, or at least it will not be fully controlled by the opposition.

When playing a man, watch his eyes, the turn of a skate, the twist of a shoulder, the movement of a knee, for each is a clue to what he may be intending

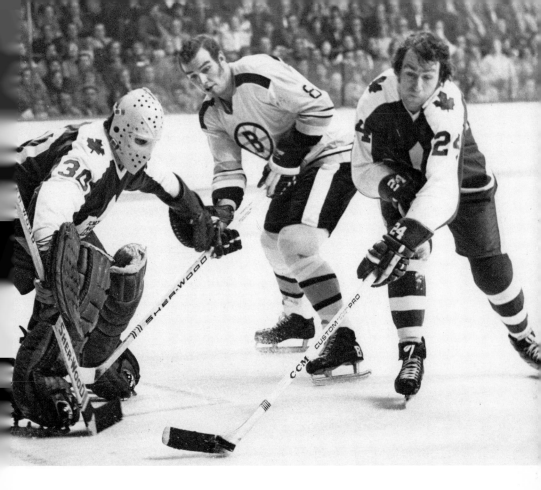

A defenseman helps the goalie protect his cage.

to do. As you spot a clue, be prepared to make a countermove.

Playing the man is sure to result in body contact. In ice hockey, the body contact gets a little energetic at times—maybe overenergetic. Tempers flare. Fists sometimes flail. Few people who have seen professional ice hockey, either in person or on television, have not witnessed occasions when two or more players drop their sticks, throw down their gloves, and go at each other with bare fists.

Fighting is not condoned, and it draws severe penalties. Fortunately, such a fracas seldom results in any real damage. Should you ever attempt fisticuffs while at the same time trying to balance yourself on a slipping and sliding pair of skate runners, you'll see why.

To have an effective defense you must be able to switch tactics the moment your team loses possession of the puck. You start out by forechecking way down in their end of the ice. You harass the man with the puck, or you stick close to the player you are supposed to guard.

And stick close means just that. Hang on to him like a hungry leech as you back-check his progress. Stay with him, as they say, even if he goes to get a drink. He is your responsibility.

If you are the center you must be doubly busy to keep the opponents from forming any kind of an attack down center ice, which is the most vulnerable

104

Fighting occurs sometimes—and draws severe penalties.

area and offers the best shooting angles at the goal.

When on defense everyone must try to keep the opponents collecting splinters along the boards. This is called "riding the man out." Above all, keep between the player and your goal.

With all this, plus the ability to feint and dodge and pass and stickhandle and check and skate and think, there is no reason why you shouldn't keep your team from being scored upon.

chapter eight
THE MAN IN THE MASK

You are called goalie. But you are also referred to as goalkeeper, goaltender, netminder, or simply as the guy who has taken on the most challenging job in sports.

By whatever name, you are the heart of your team. When all else fails, you are the last line of defense. If you fail, your team is sure to fail. If you make a couple of dozen saves during a game, your team probably will win. It's that simple.

In early days the big, hulking fellow who couldn't skate well was usually stuck in front of the goal to

In a forest of flying sticks, a goalie
makes a skate save on a bouncing puck.

plug the opening to the net. At least that kept him
out of the way of the other players. And, being big
as he was, enemy shots simply ricocheted off his slow-
moving body, arms, and legs—sometimes even off
his head.

But this is no longer true of goalies. A husky build,
a long reach, and the ability to cover a lot of space
helps. Having big and sure hands, like those of a good
baseball catcher, doesn't hurt either. More important,
however, is that you be agile as a cat, have sharp re-
flexes, perfect eyesight (with or without contact
lenses), and be cool as a skier's toes.

107

A goalie protects the crease in front of the net.

Above all, you must use your head—but not to stop pucks. You must be able to think, anticipate, and outguess your opponents.

As a goalie, you will stick to your end of the ice and guard your castle, which is that four-by-six-foot goal mouth. Also you have the crease to protect. It is your exclusive domain. And every available member of the opposing team is constantly trying to shoot hard-rubber tracer bullets past you across the crease and into the net.

You have various defensive weapons with which you attempt to stop your opponents from scoring a goal. Your skates, unlike those of your teammates, are long and flat and heavily braced. You use them often, thrusting them out in the path of a speeding puck to make a save. You have extra wide and sturdy leg pads and a chest protector, plus assorted other guards and pads. You wear a plastic mask or often a helmet and mask combination. Your stick is bigger than the other sticks, being wider and longer in the blade and wider in the shaft. You carry it in one hand, a bludgeon to deflect incoming shots. The back of your glove on the hand holding the stick has a padded shield both for protection and off which to rebound the hurtling puck.

On the other hand you wear a different kind of glove. It is very much like a first baseman's trapper mitt and is used in the same manner.

By the time you get into all of your protective gear you weigh an extra thirty pounds or so. Yet, that is not too much to tote around the small but crucially important area you patrol. At one time or another you will need all of that gear to stop, catch, or deflect the puck that comes continually at you like an angry black hornet.

During a game you will do dozens of things right. Each time you deflect the puck away with your stick

helmet

mask

suspenders

shoulder and arm pads

body pad

body and arm pads

garter belt

supporter and cup

pants

knee pads

gloves

inside leg pad

goal pads

or bounce it off your pads or snag it with your glove, you will save a goal. And the more saves you make the louder will be your acclaim.

As a goalie, also, if you make only a couple of mistakes during a game, the cheering suddenly dies. For you are allowed no leeway. A mistake on your part usually means a goal for the opponents.

You must be sure of yourself and not too quick to move. Let the other guy commit himself first. As he comes toward the goal, ragging the puck and looking for an opening, you go out to meet him. Not very far, only a few feet. Enough to fill his vision, perhaps, and achieve your all-important job of cutting down his shooting angle at the goal. But don't move so far from the net that he might deke and go around you for a shot on an unattended goal. Not enough that he can fake you out and pass off to a teammate sneaking in behind you. You can be sure that he will try to hold off and make you commit yourself before he does. It's a contest of nerves and fast reactions.

You must be the judge of how far out of the crease you can get and still protect the goal.

Keep your eye on the puck, for that is what your opponent is set upon putting past you. To watch his

Opposite: A goalie becomes a fortress on skates. **111**

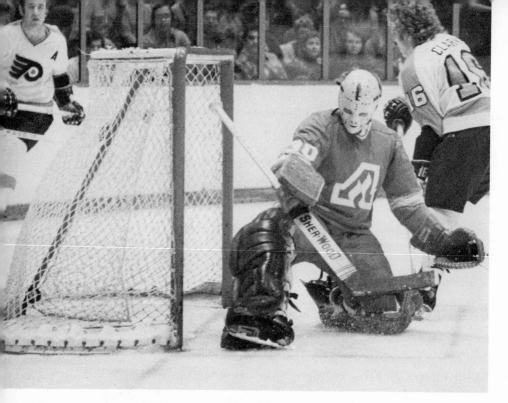

Agony! The puck bulges the net!

eyes might cause you to miss whatever clever feints he is making with his stick.

Try to know without glancing at them what your defending teammates are doing. You will need their help. No lone goalie is a fair match against a team charge. And knowing that your teammates are around to help allows you to center your attention on the primary threat—the puck.

To defend the goal, you must know exactly where

112

it is. If you are in the crease, waiting and watching an attack begin to form around center ice, sweep your stick in a quick arc, tapping each goalpost. You'll know exactly where the net is without having to look. Or you may be able to reach back with your gloved hand and feel one of the posts, planting its location in your mind.

Also, when time allows, be a caretaker of the ice in the crease. Every scramble in front of the goal leaves a residue of ice shavings, skate grooves, and other imperfections. Even a small bump or groove may deflect a hard low shot away from your stick or glove and into the net. Using the blade of your stick as

Desperately, a goalie goes out to smother the puck.

leveler and packer, keep the ice around you smooth. You can do so during the game if there is time. Always check it carefully and mend it if necessary before each period.

In taking your stance near the goal mouth, lean forward in a slight crouch. Bend your knees with your legs a little apart. The width of the leg pads will fill in the gap. Hold the stick in one hand. Grip it loosely at a fair balancing point so that despite its weight you can move it quickly in any direction. Have the blade flat on the ice for best protection against low shots.

Hold your catching glove hand up and ready. It is easier to thrust it down for a puck than to raise it up. Balanced firmly on your skates, you are set to react quickly in any direction.

Don't hang too far back in the goal mouth at any time. If you are out a few feet, there is less chance of the puck deflecting off your stick or pads and into the net. Of course, you must vary your distance with the situation. Only your experience and good judgment will tell you exactly how to defend against each charge.

It goes without saying that you should do anything and everything you can to keep that puck from getting past you and into the goal.

114

A glove save

The surest way to stop the puck is with your glove. Once you have it in the glove's netting, there is no chance for a rebound. You are the only person on your team allowed to hold the puck. When you can, it's best to drop it and clear it quickly out to one of your teammates. However, if you're not sure that a teammate will get it, hold it for a face-off. It's better to risk losing possession in a face-off than to have the puck intercepted in front of your own goal.

Stick saves, skate saves, and pad saves are more uncertain than glove saves, since an opponent may swoop in and tap the rebound into the net. But that's a chance you often have to take, for it is difficult to deflect a hard shot and to control it at the same time. On the other hand, you have every right to expect some of your teammates to be around to lend help.

When you are unable to control the puck in any other way, flop on it. Cover it up. Keep it away from probing sticks. The worst that can happen is another face-off.

Some goalies are natural floppers. Rather than

From inside the cage, a goalie tries
to get possession of a contested puck.

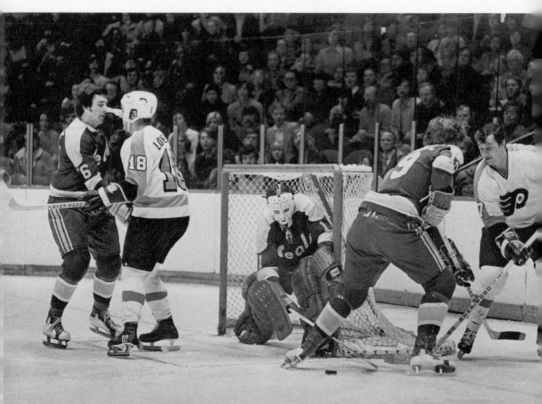

standing up and trying to block shots, they prefer to flop on the ice in front of any low-flying puck. However, when you flop you must be ready and able to bounce back up and be prepared for anything that might follow.

As a goalie there will be times when all you can see between you and the puck is a tangle of legs, clashing sticks, and prone carcasses. When down on the ice, you will often make an instant check of the colors of the socks around you to determine whether you are

A goalie's nightmare!

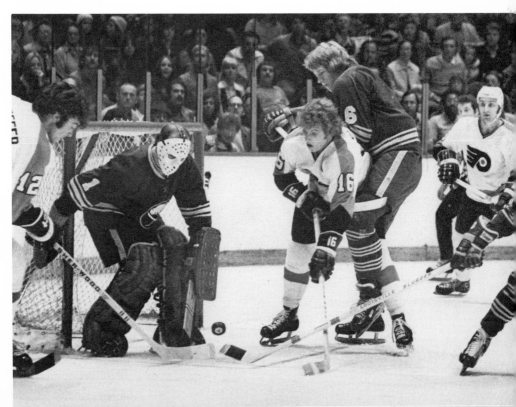

surrounded by friends or foes. But, above all, you must keep your eyes focused on that little rubber disc, which at any moment may emerge from the melee, streaking for the goal mouth.

Stay alert for such screen shots or for flip shots, high shots or low shots, down the center and in the corners. At times you will be faced with one- or two-man breakaways.

There will be just you, your various pads and implements, and your courage standing off a sure goal —perhaps the game. Your motto should always be "They shall not pass!"

chapter nine
THE HAT TRICK

It happens all the time. You learn the fundamentals of the game, you practice hard, and now you are trembling like a bird dog waiting for the call to take to the ice.

You line up with your teammates near the gate. The metallic voice of the loudspeaker announces your name. Your friends in the crowd yell. Nervous, but eager, you make your little jump out onto the ice . . .

. . . and take a pratfall!

It can't happen to you? It happened recently to a world-famous player in the annual all-star game.

Hockey is that kind of a game, full of surprises and frustrations. You train and get yourself into the top physical condition the game demands. You master the basics of skating and stickhandling. Then you charge out onto the ice, but nothing seems to work the way you had planned.

Why not? Well, in what other game do the players maneuver on a pair of knifelike blades on slippery surface? Even staying on your feet is difficult. And with a swarm of opponents bent upon knocking you off your skates, the problems double.

Ice hockey is a game of mistakes. The team that makes the fewest usually wins. Most often it's the team that has paid the greatest attention to training and practice.

You may find yourself playing on soft ice or on a rink where the boards are soggy, and you can't bank a decent pass around the corner. You may lose your footing often, or an unusual number of your passes may be intercepted. But you can't fuss and fume over mishaps. You still must rely upon the fundamentals you have learned and make your moves automatically.

In time, despite ragged ice or splintery boards, your steady play will pay off.

120

When things are going wrong and your confidence wavers, don't let your opponents sense your despair. They may start trying to run you, and if you let them, you might as well hang up your skates. Hockey is a game that takes doggedness and guts.

A play unfolds. You shoot your stick out for a pass, but it glances off and is snagged by the opposition. Desperately you lunge for it—and trip the puck carrier. Two-minute penalty. But it wasn't deliberate! If your coach is good, he will use a "rubber needle" —tell you how you could have avoided the tripping infraction (as if you didn't know!)—but he'll let it go at that and not rub it in.

Anyone who plays or coaches ice hockey knows that despite the best-laid plans, most goals are scored out of wild scrambles around the crease. This does not mean that planned strategy is not important.

What it does mean is that you must always be alert for the unexpected opportunity—a loose puck, a rebound, a chance to deflect a wild shot into the net. The nature of the game is to expect the unexpected and to make the best of it.

Despite the frustrations—the pratfalls, losing the elusive puck, getting pinned against the boards,

checked out from under your helmet, or otherwise de-
railed from your purpose—once you have played ice
hockey, you'll find other sports as tame as checkers.
Indeed, there are more challenges in ice hockey than
in nearly any game you can think of.

Ice hockey is a special kind of contest that takes a
certain breed of guy to play. You need to be aggressive. You must have the patience and determination
to learn the fundamentals, be willing to practice hard,
and possess a strong desire to win.

If you fill this bill, hockey is your game.

You've scored the hat trick!

Ice hockey is sports competition at its highest peak.

glossary

Attacking zone—area between the opponent's blue line and his goal.
Back-check—to try to recapture puck from opponents as they move toward your defending zone.
Backskate—to skate backwards.
Banana blade—curved hockey stick blade.
Biscuit—slang for puck.
Boarding—a major infraction caused by smashing an opponent into the boards.
Boards—wooden wall surrounding the ice rink.
Breakaway—the puck carrier outrushes the defenders toward their goal.
Center zone—area between the two blue lines.
Charging—moving more than two strides to slam into an opposing player.

Clear the puck—move the puck away from the vicinity of your own goal.

Crease—the four-by-eight-foot rectangle in front of the goal.

Defending zone—area from your blue line to your goal.

Deke—to fake an opponent into committing himself first.

Digger—an aggressive player who keeps after the puck.

Draw—*see* Face-off.

Face-off—an official drops the puck between the sticks of two opposing players to start play.

Flopper—a goalie who often falls to the ice in order to block a shot on goal.

Forecheck—to harass opponents when they have the puck near their own goal.

Forwards—center and left and right wingmen.

Freeze the puck—to pin the puck against the boards with stick or skates, forcing a face-off.

Garbage man—slang for a player who hovers around the opponent's goal crease, ready to tap in a rebound or loose puck.

Goal—one point scored by shooting the puck through the goal mouth; also the netted structure into which the puck is shot.

Goalie (goalkeeper, goaltender, netminder)—player stationed in front of the goal to guard against the other team's scoring.

Goal mouth—the 4-by-6-foot opening to the goal cage.

Hat trick—for one player to score three goals in a single game.

Headmanning—passing to a teammate nearer to the opponent's goal.

Hockey stop—to brake quickly by twisting and digging skates into the ice at a ninety-degree angle to the direction of travel.

Icing—shooting or passing the puck from behind the center line over the opponent's goal line.

Interference—to check an opposing player without the puck.

Jump stop—similar to hockey stop, except done with a jump and twist.

124

Lie—the angle of the blade of a hockey stick to the shaft.

Line—*see* Forwards.

Net—*see* Goal.

Neutral zone—*see* Center zone.

Offside—when a player is illegally in advance of the puck.

Penalty box—an off-ice seating area where players serve their time for committing rule infractions.

Penalty killers—forwards particularly skilled at playing defense while their team is shorthanded.

Penalty shot—a one-on-one shot attempt against an opposing goalie awarded following flagrant interference with a goal-ward-bound player.

Points—positions just inside the blue line taken by the players of the attacking team farthest from the goal.

Power play—a full five-man attack when opponents are short-handed.

Puck—a vulcanized rubber disc 1 inch thick and 3 inches in diameter, weighing 5½ to 6 ounces.

Radius—the amount of upward curve in a skate blade.

Ragging the puck—*see* Stickhandle.

Riding the man out—crowding the puck carrier toward the boards.

Rockering—*see* Radius.

Save—when a goalie prevents the scoring of a goal.

Shot—a try for goal.

Sin bin—*see* Penalty box.

Slot—area directly in front of goal.

Split the defense—a puck handler manages to skate between two opposing defensemen.

Stickhandling—deft stick control of the puck to outmaneuver and confound the opposition.

Zone infraction—to cross the blue line into your attacking zone ahead of the puck.

index

indicates illustrations

Back-checking, 89*, 90, 104
Boards, 14, 17, 53-54, 73, 78, 80, 89, 96, 102, 120
Body checks, 73-74, 79-80, 90-92, 91*, 96
  hip, 73, 89, 91
  shoulder, 73, 90
Breakaway, 44, 60-61*, 118
Center, 13, 74, 77
Crease, 17, 62, 108*, 111, 113
Defense, 74, 87-105, 95*
Defenseman, 13, 74, 76, 77, 78, 79-80, 82-83, 84, 103*
Deke, 66, 84, 94, 99, 111

Draw, *see* Face-off
Face-off, 17, 19, 22-23, 62, 72-73*, 81, 95, 101, 115, 116
Forechecking, 88*-90, 104
Forwards, 13, 74, 76, 88, 92
Goal (the net), 16*, 17, 62, 107, 112*, 113, 114
  mouth, 17, 35, 114, 118
  post, 17, 113
Goalkeeper, 13, 17, 76, 77, 78-79, 80, 103*, 106-118, 107*, 108*, 113*, 115*, 116*, 117*
  protective gear, 109, 110*

126

skates, 108-109
stick, 37, 109
Hat trick, 71, 122
History of game, 11-13
Infractions, 19, 22, 83-84,
95-102, 104
boarding, 20, 22
butt-ending, 97, 99*
charging, 20, 96
cross-checking, 20, 98, 100*
fighting, 104, 105*
high-sticking, 97
hooking, 20, 96, 97*
icing, 19
interference, 96
offside, 19, 48
slashing, 97
spearing, 20, 97, 98*
stick throwing, 98-99
zone, 17
Line, *see* Forwards
Mighty Mites, 13
National Hockey League, 13
Offense, 72-86, 75*
Passes
back, 53, 55*, 78
carom, 53-54*
deflection, 55-56
drop, 52-53
flip, 50-52, 84
headmanning, 48, 76
sweep (flat), 48, 49*, 50
wrist (snap or push), 50, 84

Passing, 46-59, 47*, 51*,
53*, 57*
Penalties, 19, 22, 86, 95-102,
104
Penalty box, 19, 22, 84,
95-96, 98
Penalty killer, 84, 101-102
Penalty shot, 99-100
Physical conditioning, 23
Plan of game, 76-86, 77*
Points, 82-83
Pollywogs, 13
Protective clothing, 19-20, 21*
Puck, control of, 28*-29*
Receiving, 56-59, 57*
Rink, 14-17, 15*
Rules of game, 14, 17-19,
83-84, 94-95
Save, 77, 107*, 111, 113*,
115*-116
Shot on goal, 60-71*, 78-79,*
83, 84-86, 85*
Shots
backhand, 65*, 66
flip, 63-65, 64*, 118
forehand, 66
screen, 118
slap, 35, 66-70, 67*, 71*,
78
wrist, 61-63*, 65
Skates, 24-27
blades, 25*, 26
radius, 26

Skating, 24-33, 27*
   crossover step, 33
   double-leg stop, 31-32*
   hockey stop, 30
   jump stop, 31-32
   single-leg stop, 30-31
Slot, 84
Stick
   banana blade, 37, 38*
   holding of, 39-41*
   lie of, 35-37, 36*

   selection of, 34-39, 36*
   taping of, 38-39
Stick checks, 90, 92
   hook, 92*, 93
   poke, 43, 89, 92
   sweep, 93, 94*
Stickhandling, 34-45, 42*, 44*
Substitution, 22, 75
Time-outs, 22
Wingman, 13, 74, 77, 78-79
World Hockey Association, 13